The Life of Mozart

Prose Series 15

Stendhal

The Life of Mozart

Translated from the French by
Daniel Sloate

Guernica

Montreal, 1991

Original Title:
Vie de Mozart

Copyright © Guernica Editions Inc and Daniel Sloate, 1991.
All right reserved.

This translation was based on *Vie de Mozart* by Stendhal as
published in 1990 by Les Éditions Climats
(Castelnau-le-Lez, France).

Antonio D'Alfonso, publisher-editor
Guernica Editions Inc.
P.O. Box 633, Station N.D.G.
Montreal (Quebec), Canada H4A 3R1

Canadian Cataloguing in Publication Data
Stendhal, 1783-1842
The Life of Mozart

(Prose series; 15)
Translation of: La vie de Mozart.
ISBN 0-920717-59-4

1. Mozart, Wolfgang Amadeus, 1756-1791.
2. Composers–Austria–Biography. I. Title II. series.

ML410.M9S82513 1991   780'.92   C91-090231-3

Venice, July 21, 1814.

You expressed a wish, my good friend, to read something on the life of Mozart. I inquired as to the best possible sources for this famous man and had patience enough to translate for you from the German the biography by Adolph Heinrich von Schlichtengroll. I was impressed by its candour. I now submit it to you and ask you to excuse the simplicity of its appearance.

Chapter I

Mozart's Childhood

Mozart's father had a profound influence on the singular destiny of his son to the extent, perhaps, of developing and modifying his talents. For this reason it is important to say a few words about Leopold Mozart.

Mozart's father was a bookbinder in Augsburg. He studied in Salzburg and in 1743 was admitted into the group of court musicians of the archbishop of Salzburg. In 1762 he became assistant kappelmeister to the archbishop. As his duties did not take up all his time, he gave music and violin lessons. He even published a work entitled *A Treatise on the Fundamental Problems of Violin Playing*, which enjoyed much success. He married Anna Maria Pertl, and it was noted, as a circumstance of interest to the careful observer, that the parents of an artist born with such genius for music were singled out by the inhabitants of Salzburg for their rare physical beauty.

Of the seven children born of this union, only two survived: a daughter, Maria Anna, and a son, the subject of this biography. Joannes Chrysostomus Wolfgangus Theophilus Mozart was born in Salzburg on

January 27, 1756. A few years later, Mozart's father gave up teaching private lessons and decided to devote himself to the musical education of his two children. Maria Anna, a little older than Wolfgang, drew much profit from these lessons and, on the tours she and her family made later, she shared some of the admiration aroused by her brother's talent. Eventually she married a counsellor to the archbishop of Salzburg, preferring domestic tranquillity to the fame that goes with great talent.

Mozart was about three years old when his father began to give harpsichord lessons to his sister, who was seven. Mozart's amazing gifts for music were immediately apparent. He loved to look for thirds on the piano and was delighted whenever he found a pleasing progression. I would like to give some specific details which I think will interest the reader.

When Mozart was four years old, his father started to teach him, almost like playing a game, a few minuets and other musical pieces. The occupation was as pleasant for the teacher as it was for the pupil. It took Mozart half an hour to learn how to play a minuet, and scarcely twice that time to learn a longer piece. He would play them immediately afterwards quite accurately and with the right tempo. He made such swift progress that at the age of five years, he was already inventing little pieces that he would play for his father and which, to encourage the nascent talent of his son, Leopold would kindly transcribe.

Before Mozart became interested in music, he had been very fond of the games and diversions of a child of his age, sometimes to the point of missing meals when something amused him enough. On all these occasions, he showed his sensitive and loving nature. He would often say, sometimes as frequently as a dozen times a day, to the people around him 'Do you like me?' and whenever someone teasingly answered no, tears would immediately come to his eyes. From the moment he became interested in music, however, his fondness for the amusements of his age vanished, or they had to be associated with music to arouse his attention. A friend of the family often played with him, and they would carry toys in a procession from one room to another; whichever one happened to have nothing in his hands would play a marching tune on the violin.

For some months, his interest in the usual studies of childhood absorbed Mozart so completely that he ignored everything else, even music. While he was learning arithmetic, he would scribble chalk figures on chairs, tables, walls, and even on the floors. His keen mind was fascinated by every new object that came into his ken. But he turned his attention once again to music and made such remarkable progress that his father, who was always at his side and could observe his son closely, came to look upon him as a genius.

The following eye-witness account will illustrate what has just been related. Mozart's father came back one day from church with one of his friends and found his son busily writing.

'What are you doing, my son?' he asked.

'I'm composing a concerto for harpsichord. I've almost finished the first part.'

'Let's have a look at all that fine scribbling.'

'Not just yet if you don't mind; I haven't quite finished.'

But his father took the paper from him and showed it to his friend: the page was a maze of notes that were barely decipherable because of the ink blots scattered everywhere. The two friends had a good laugh as they stared at the messy paper, but soon Mozart's father looked more closely and before long his eyes filled with tears of joy and admiration.

'Look here,' he said to his friend with a smile and a catch in his voice, 'everything has been composed according to the rules. It's too bad we can't use this piece because it's too difficult, and no one could ever possibly play it.'

Mozart answered, 'It's a concerto and you have to study it to know how to play it properly. Let me show you how it should be played.'

He started to play the piece but was unable to proceed far enough to show the others what his ideas were. At that time, the young Mozart was firmly convinced that playing a concerto and performing a miracle were one and the same. The composition just mentioned was a series of notes put down quite accurately, but which presented so many difficulties that the most gifted musician would have found it impossible to play them.

Mozart's father was so amazed by his son's gifts that he decided to exhibit him and share his admiration with the rest of the world. The idea was nothing extraordinary at the time. As soon as Wolfgang had reached the age of six years, the Mozart family, comprising father, mother, Maria Anna and Wolfgang travelled to Munich. The two children, who were showered with praise by everyone, played for the Elector. This first tour was a complete success. Back in Salzburg, and thrilled with their reception, the young virtuosos set to work with even more zeal and attained such a degree of mastery of the piano that their tender age was no longer the remarkable thing about their talent. During the fall of 1762, the whole family travelled to Vienna where the children played at the court.

On that occasion, the Emperor Francis I said jokingly to little Wolfgang, 'Playing with all your fingers is easy; but playing with one finger, and on a harpsichord with the keyboard concealed, there is a true challenge.'

Without appearing in the least surprised by this strange proposal, Mozart immediately began playing with one finger, clearly and accurately. He requested a cloth be placed over the keyboard, and then continued playing as though he had always played in that fashion.

From a very early age, Mozart had a profound sense of pride in his musical abilities and his head was never turned by the praise he received from great people. When his audience comprised persons who knew little about music, he would play trifling pieces for them. When, however, he was in the company of connoisseurs, he would play with all the fire and concentration at his disposal; often his father resorted to subterfuges and would pass off important people before whom his son was to perform as musical connoisseurs. When Mozart, at the age of six, was about to play the harpsichord before the Emperor Francis, he addressed his majesty thus: 'Why isn't Mr. Wagensei here? He's the one who should be here. He knows music.'

The Emperor summoned Wagensei and gave him his own seat next to the harpsichord.

'Sir,' said Mozart to the composer, 'I'm playing one of your concertos and you will have to turn the pages for me.'

Mozart had always played the harpsichord up to that time, and his extraordinary skill on that instrument seemed to preclude any idea of his studying any other. But his genius was such that it surpassed anything anyone could dare hope: he did not even need to take lessons.

When he came back to Salzburg from Vienna with his parents, he was carrying a little violin that had been given to him during his stay in the capital and which gave him much pleasure and amusement. Shortly after the family's return, a certain Wenzl, a gifted violinist, and who was beginning his career as a composer, came to see Leopold Mozart. Wenzl wanted his opinion on six trios he had composed while the Mozart family had been in Vienna. Schachtner, a trumpet player in the archbishop's orchestra and someone whom the young Mozart was fond of, happened to be at Mozart's house at the time and we will let him speak.

'Leopold was to play the bass part,' Schachtner said, 'Wenzl was to take the first violin part and I was to play the second violin. Wolfgang asked if he might be allowed to play the second violin part instead of me but his father scolded him for his childish request and told him he could not possibly play since he had not taken any violin lessons. His son answered he saw no reason why he had to take lessons to play the second violin part. Wolfgang's father was somewhat annoyed at his son's answer, and bade him go away and not bother us again. Wolfgang was so upset that he burst into tears. He started away with his little violin in his hand but I stopped him and requested that he be allowed to play along with me, to which his father gave grudging consent. Leopold told his son that he might play with me on the condition he play very quietly and not be heard above the rest of us, and that if he did not comply, he would be summarily dismissed. We began the trio and Wolfgang played along with me but it was not long before I realised to my great astonishment that my own playing was perfectly superfluous. I said not a word and, putting down my violin, I looked over at Wolfgang's father. Leopold was weeping, deeply moved by what had just happened. The child continued playing and went through the six trios. Our praises made him bold enough to claim that he could play the first violin part just as well, and so for the sport of it we let him try. We had a good laugh as we listened to him play the part, which he did in irregular fashion to be sure but never was he caught short.'

Each day brought more proof of Mozart's extraordinary talent for music. He was capable of distinguishing and picking out the slightest differences between sounds; any note that was false or merely harsh and unpleasant was torture to him. All through his tender childhood, and until he was ten years old, the trumpet filled him with utter terror unless it was played as accompaniment to a piece of music. Whenever he was near a trumpet, he reacted in much the same way some children react when a loaded pistol is aimed in jest at them. His father thought he would cure his son of his dread by sounding the trumpet in his presence despite his son's pleas for mercy; the first note caused Wolfgang to turn pale and collapse; had the playing not ceased immediately, the boy would almost certainly have gone into convulsions.

Once he had proved his talent on the violin, Mozart would sometimes use Schachtner's instrument and would extract the sweetest of sounds from it, much to Schachtner's delight and admiration. One day, the latter arrived at the Mozart home while Wolfgang was playing his own violin. When Schachtner began to play, the child asked, 'What has happened to your violin?' and he went on playing fantasies. Then, after reflecting a few moments, he said to Schachtner, 'Why couldn't you leave your violin tuned the same way it was when I last used it? It is one-eighth of a note lower than the violin I'm holding.'

At first everyone laughed at Mozart's extreme exactitude, but his father, who had already had several opportunities to observe his son's extraordinary ability to remember tones, asked to inspect the violin. To everyone's great astonishment, it was tuned one-eighth of a note lower than the violin Mozart was holding.

Even though each new day brought further demonstrations of the child's gifts and the awe-struck admiration they produced in others, Mozart did not turn arrogant or conceited. Where his talent was concerned, he was a man; in every other respect he was a child, obliging and obedient. He never showed any displeasure at his father's demands on him. Even on days when he had played continuously for others, he would not display the slightest annoyance and would go on playing if that was his father's wish. The most subtle of signals sent out by his parents were understood and executed by him and his sense of obedience was so strong that he would refuse candies unless he had been given permission to accept them. Mozart was seven years old when his family went on an extended tour.

It was in July of 1763, and this date marks the beginning of Mozart's renown in Europe. The tour began in Munich where the young virtuoso played a fantasy and a violin concerto for the Elector. Receiving the highest acclaim possible, the two children gave public concerts or played for princes in Augsburg, Mannheim, Frankfurt, Coblenz and Brussels. They arrived in Paris in November and stayed five months. They performed at Versailles where Mozart played the organ in the king's chapel for the court. In Paris they gave two grand concerts and were highly acclaimed by everyone. A portrait, after a drawing by Carmontelle, was painted in their honour, showing Leopold with his two children. It was in Paris that the young Mozart composed and published his first works. He dedicated the first one to Madame Victoire, the second daughter of Louis XV, and the second one to the Comtesse de Tessé.

The Mozart family crossed over to England in April of 1764, and remained there until almost the middle of the following year. The children performed before the king, and as he had done at Versailles, Mozart played the organ in the royal chapel. More praise was showered on his organ playing than on his prowess at the harpsichord. He and his sister gave a grand concert where all the symphonies were of his own composition. One can well imagine that the two children, and especially Wolfgang, were not content to remain at the level of excellence that, day after day, incited much flattering praise, nor did they allow their continuous travels to interrupt their daily schedule of regular work. They started to play concertos for two harpsichords in London, and Wolfgang also began singing arias, which he did with much feeling. In London and Paris, some disbelievers presented him with various difficult passages from the masters such as Bach and Haendel; Mozart always played them instantly at first glance and with the greatest accuracy imaginable.

One day, in the presence of the king of England, he was given a ground bass and skilfully turned it into a superb melody. On another occasion, the queen's music master, Johann Christian Bach, took little Mozart on his lap and played a few bars. Wolfgang picked up where Christian had left off, and they continued to alternate as they played an entire sonata; they did so with such precision that those who could not see them playing together were convinced there was only one person performing.

During his stay in England, when he was eight years old, Wolfgang composed six sonatas which he published in London and dedicated to the queen.

In July of the year 1765, the Mozart family was back in Calais, and from there they continued on through Flanders where the young virtuoso often performed on the organ in churches, monasteries and cathedrals along their way. In The Hague, both children fell very seriously ill and it was feared they might not recover. It took them four months to get well; during Wolfgang's convalescence, he composed six sonatas for the piano which he dedicated to the princess of Nassau-Weilbourg. The family spent the beginning of 1766 in Amsterdam and thence to The Hague to attend the installation of the prince of Orange. To mark the solemn occasion, Wolfgang composed a *quodlibet* for the instruments of the orchestra, and various airs and variations for the princess.

After performing several times for the *stathouder*, they came back to Paris where they spent two months. They finally returned to Germany via Lyons and Switzerland. In Munich, the Elector proposed a musical theme to Wolfgang and asked him to develop it and write it down on the spot. He did so while the prince looked on, and without resorting to the harpsichord or the violin. When he had finished writing it down, he played it, which aroused the greatest astonishment in the Elector and the entire court.

They returned to Salzburg around the end of November, 1768, after an absence of more than three years; they remained in that city until the fall of the following year; Mozart seemed to be less restless and his gifts seemed to have doubled. In 1768, the children played in Vienna in the presence of the Emperor Joseph II who commissioned the young Mozart to compose the music for an opera buffa. This was to be *La Finta semplice*; it was approved by Hasse the kappelmeister and by Metastasio, but it was not performed in the theatre. On several occasions, in the presence of the kappelmeister Hasse or Bono, Metastasio, the Duke of Braganza, Prince Kaunitz, Mozart's father would give his son the first Italian air he could lay his hand on and Wolfgang would compose the music for each instrument as those in attendance looked on. At the inauguration of the Church of the Orphans, he composed the music for the mass, a motet, and a duo for trumpets. Even though he was only twelve years old at the time, he conducted this solemn music in the presence of the imperial court.

He came back and spent the year 1769 in Salzburg. His father took him to Italy in December. One can easily imagine the enthusiastic reception that Italy gave to this famous child who had aroused such admiration in other parts of Europe.

The setting for his triumph in Milan was the residence of the governor general, Count Firmian. After receiving the text of the opera that was to be performed during the carnival of 1771, and for which Wolfgang was to compose the music, he left Milan in March of 1770. In Bologna, he met a most ardent admirer in the person of the renowned Padre Martini, the same man Jomelli had come to study with. Padre Martini and the music lovers of Bologna were thrilled at the sight of this child, small for his age, and looking even younger than his thirteen years, as he developed all the fugal themes proposed by Padre Martini and played them flawlessly and without hesitation on the piano. The precision of his playing aroused the same wonderment in Florence where he played at sight the most difficult themes and fugues proposed to him by the Marquis de Ligneville, a famous music lover.

I have a non-musical anecdote to relate about his stay in Florence. It was there that Mozart met a young English boy of fourteen named Thomas Linley. He was a pupil of Martini's, and the boy played the violin with superb grace and agility. The friendship between the two boys grew very strong. When the time came for their separation, Linley presented Mozart with a set of verses he had ordered for the occasion from the renowned Corilla. He accompanied Wolfgang's coach to the city, where the two children, weeping abundantly, parted from each other.

Leopold and his son travelled to Rome for Holy Week. We are not surprised to learn they made a point of going to the Sistine Chapel on Holy Wednesday to hear the choir sing the famous *Miserere*. It was said at the time that no musician of the pope, on pain of excommunication, was permitted to give a copy of the *Miserere* to anyone, and so Mozart decided to memorize it. He copied it down once he was back in his rooms.

The *Miserere* was sung again on Holy Friday, and Mozart attended once more; he concealed the manuscript from view with his hat and was thus able to make a few corrections. This anecdote caused a sensation throughout the city. The Romans were somewhat sceptical of the whole thing, and requested that Wolfgang sing the *Miserere* at a concert. He did so to everyone's delight. The castrato Cristofori, who had sung the piece at the Sistine and who was present at the concert, made Mozart's triumph complete by the utter amazement he displayed.

Mozart's accomplishment in this case is even more extraordinary than one would at first imagine. I beg the reader's indulgence for the following details I would like to give about the Sistine Chapel and the *Miserere*.

Ordinarily, there are at least thirty-two singers in the Chapel choir. No organ or instrument of any kind is used to accompany them. The Sistine Chapel reached its highest renown as an institution in the early years of the eighteenth century. Since then, the salaries of the choir members have remained nominally the same, that is, low compared to salaries of the best singers of operatic roles as the opera gained in popu-

23

larity. For this reason, the Sistine no longer has the pick of the most talented artists.

The *Miserere* that is sung twice in the Sistine Chapel during Holy Week, and which has such a singular effect on visitors, was composed about two hundred years ago by Gregorio Allegri, a descendant of Antonio Allegri, better known under the name of Correggio. When the *Miserere* starts, the pope and the cardinals prostrate themselves: the tapers cast their light on the Last Judgment that Michelangelo painted on the wall behind the altar. As the *Miserere* proceeds, the tapers are extinguished one by one; the faces of all the wretched figures that Michelangelo painted with such terrible energy become even more dramatic in the pale glow of the last remaining tapers. When the *Miserere* is about to finish, the kappelmeister, who is conducting, slows down the tempo imperceptibly, and the singers lower the volume of their voices so the music slowly fades away; the sinner, overwhelmed by the majesty of his God, and prostrate before His throne, seems to be waiting silently for the voice of his Judge to be heard.

The sublime effect of this music seems to me to be dependent on the manner in which it is sung and on the place where it is executed. Tradition has taught the pope's singers certain ways of projecting their voices to the greatest advantage possible; this effect cannot be expressed by the musical notes themselves. The choristers sing in such a way that their voices superbly imbue the music with feeling. The same melody is repeated for each verse of the psalm, but although the music is similar on the whole, it is subtly different in the details. It is thus easily retained, and yet is not tedious. The technique of the Sistine choir is to speed up or slow down the tempo for certain words, to increase or decrease the sounds according to the meaning of the words, and to sing certain complete verses faster than others.

Now we come to what we meant when we said how incredible Mozart's tour de force was by singing the *Miserere*. The Emperor Leopold I, who loved music and was a good composer in his own right, requested, through his ambassador, that the pope send him a copy of the *Miserere* for performance in the imperial chapel of Vienna, and the request was granted. The kappelmeister of the Sistine made the copy and dispatched it to the emperor, who had the best singers of the time in his service.

Despite the talents of these singers, however, the effect of the *Miserere* on the Viennese court was similar to that of a musical instrument played out of tune. The emperor and his court suspected that the pope's kappelmeister, intent on keeping the *Miserere* for himself, had evaded the pope's orders by sending along an utterly banal composition. The emperor immediately sent a messenger to complain to the pope about the lack of respect to his person. The kappelmeister was dismissed without the pope, in his indignation, deigning to hear his explanation. The poor kappelmeister, however, did manage to get a cardinal to intercede for him and explain to the pope that the manner in which the music should be performed was not expressed in the notes, and could only be acquired after years of practice under the tutorship of the Sistine choir masters who had tradition on their side. His Holiness, not a musician, was hard put to understand how the same notes in Rome did not have the same value in Vienna. Nevertheless, he ordered the poor kappelmeister to draft a defence that would be sent to the emperor, and in due time the kappelmeister reingratiated himself with the pope.

This well-known anecdote was present in the minds of the Romans as they watched a child singing their *Miserere* flawlessly after only two lessons; and nothing is more difficult, in the realm of the arts, than to arouse surprise and wonder in the Romans.

All reputations diminish dramatically in the city of Rome, where beautiful things of every sort are the rule.

I do not know whether it was because of the success he enjoyed with the *Miserere*, but apparently the solemn melancholy of that music made a deep and lasting impression on Mozart's soul. Ever afterwards, he showed a marked preference for the music of Haendel and tender Boccherini.

Chapter II
Mozart's Childhood Continued

The Mozart family left Rome for Naples, where Wolfgang played the piano at the *Conservatorio alla pielà*. As he was playing a sonata, the audience decided he must be wearing a magic ring; Mozart finally realised what they were shouting about and he removed his ring. One can imagine the effect on persons this superstitious when the music was just as beautiful once the ring was gone. Wolfgang gave another grand concert at the residence of Prince Kaunitz, the emperor's ambassador, and then returned to Rome. The pope wanted to see him, and bestowed on him the Cross of the Order of the Golden Spur (*auratae Militiae eques*). In Bologna, he was honoured with election to a membership in the Academia Philharmonica. According to the custom, he was confined to a room by himself and in less than half an hour he had composed an antiphon for four voices.

Leopold Mozart was anxious to return to Milan so his son could work on the opera he had been commissioned to write. Time was running out. The Mozarts did not arrive until nearly the end of October, 1770. Had

it not been for the promise made by Wolfgang, he could have obtained what is considered in Italy to be the highest honour for
a musician, namely to be asked to write an
opera seria for the theatre in Rome.

On December 26, the first performance
of *Mitridate* was given in Milan; Mozart was
fourteen years of age when he composed it.
The opera was given more than twenty consecutive performances. Its success can be
gauged by the fact the impresario signed
Mozart to a contract for the composition of
the first opera of the 1773 season. Wolfgang
left Milan to great acclaim, and headed for
Venice and the final days of the carnival. In
Verona, which he merely travelled through,
he was made a member of the Philharmonic
Society of that city. He was received
throughout Italy in the most distinguished
fashion imaginable; he was referred to as *il
cavaliere filarmonico* by everyone.

In March of 1771 when Mozart returned
with his father to Salzburg, a letter from
Count Firmian of Milan was waiting for
him; it requested, in the name of the
Empress Maria Theresa, that Mozart compose a serenade for the wedding of the
Archduke Ferdinand. The empress had cho-
sen the renowned Hasse, as the oldest of the
kappelmeister, to compose the opera, and
she wanted the youngest composer to write

a serenade, the title of which was *Ascanio in Alba*. Wolfgang promised to undertake the task, and left for Milan in August, where alternate performances of the opera and the serenade were given during the wedding celebrations.

In 1772, he composed a serenade entitled *Il Sogno di Scipione* for the election of the new archbishop of Salzburg. The following winter was spent in Milan where he composed *Lucio Silla*, an opera seria, which had twenty-six consecutive performances. In the spring of 1773, Mozart was back in Salzburg. In that year and the following one, Mozart made a few trips with his father to Vienna and Munich; they provided him with the opportunity to compose several excellent scores, among them an opera buffa entitled *La Finta giardiniera*, and two masses for the chapel of the Elector of Bavaria. In 1775, the Archduke Maximilian spent some time in Salzburg, and it was on that occasion that Mozart composed an opera entitled *Il Re pastore*.

The most extraordinary part of Mozart's life is his childhood; its details will surely be of pleasurable interest to the philosopher and the artist. We will be more concise when talking about the rest of his all too brief life.

Chapter III

At nineteen years of age, Mozart could well believe he had attained the pinnacle of his art since everyone from London to Naples told him so. His good fortune and renown made him one of the most sought-after musicians by the great cities of Europe. Experience proved that he could count on the public's acclaim wherever he went. His father decided that Paris was the city which suited him best, and in September of 1777, he set out for Paris accompanied by his mother.

There is little doubt that it would have been quite advantageous for him had he decided to stay there, but there were several reasons why he did not. First, French music of the period did not appeal to him; secondly, the popularity of vocal music at the time would not have given him much chance to compose for musical instruments; and lastly, in the following year, his mother died. From that moment onward, his stay in Paris became unbearable. After composing a symphony and a few other pieces for the Concert Spirituel, he hastened to return to his father's side at the beginning of 1779.

In November of the following year, he went to Vienna where his sovereign, the archbishop of Salzburg, had summoned him. He was twenty-four years old. His stay in Vienna was most pleasing to him, but apparently the beauties of Vienna even more so. What is definite is the fact he decided to remain in that city and nothing could ever induce him to leave. Mozart's great sensitivity and his supreme mastery of his art were now exposed to life's myriad emotions. It was not long before he became the century's most beloved composer and a rare example of the child prodigy who grew up to be a great man.[1]

It would be long and difficult to proceed to a specific analysis of Mozart's works, and in any case music lovers must know them all anyway. Most of his operas were written in Vienna and enjoyed great success in that city. One of them, however, was particularly loved: *The Magic Flute*, which was produced one hundred times in less than a year.

Like Raphaël, Mozart encompassed the whole range of his art. There was only one thing that Raphaël seemed unable to grasp: the way to paint figures directly on a ceiling without having recourse to subterfuges such as painting his subjects on a canvas attached to the ceiling, or held in place by allegorical figures.

As for Mozart, I see no musical genre in which he did not excel. His operas, symphonies, songs, *airs de danse* were all touched with greatness. Baron Van Sweiten, Haydn's friend, went so far as to state that if Mozart had lived longer, he would have snatched the sceptre of instrumental music from Haydn's grasp. In the opera buffa genre, Mozart lacked a certain gaiety and in this respect he is not up to the excellence of a Galuppi, a Guglielmi, or a Sarti.

The qualities that impress one in his music, aside from his genius, involve a fresh approach to the use of the orchestra, and especially the wind instruments. He uses the flute, which Cimarosa seldom used, to great advantage. He includes the full range of beautiful sounds found in the symphony in all his accompaniments.

Mozart has been criticized for knowing no other music but his own and showing little interest in the compositions of others. This kind of petty reproach surely springs from wounded vanity. Mozart was busy writing down his ideas all his life, and for this reason had little time to peruse the compositions of others. But he was frankly generous with his praise whenever he came across something good, even the simplest of songs, as long as it was original. Nevertheless, he was much less diplomatic than the great artists of Italy, and whenever he heard something mediocre his disdain was inexorable.

He had great esteem for Porpora, Durante, Leo, and Alexander Scarlatti but he placed Haendel above everyone else. He knew the major works of this great master by heart.

'More so than any of us,' Mozart would say, 'Haendel understands best how to achieve the greatest effects. When he decides to do so, the result is like a thunderbolt.'

He had the following to say about Jomelli: 'This artist is brilliant in certain domains and will remain so, but he should not have left them for other domains nor should he have tried to write sacred music in the old style.'

He was not an admirer of Vincenzo Martini whose *Cosa rara* was very popular at the time. 'There are some very nice things in the music,' he said, 'but in twenty years from now, no one will remember them.' Mozart has left nine operas with Italian libretti: *La Finta semplice*, his first attempt in the opera buffa genre; *Mitridate, Il Re de Ponto* and *Lucio Silla*, both in the opera seria genre; *La Finta giardiniera*, an opera buffa, *Idomeneo*, an opera seria; *Le Nozze di Figaro*, composed in 1786, and *Don Giovanni* in 1787; *Così fan tutte*, an opera buffa; *La Clemenza di Tito* with a libretto by Metastasio, performed in 1791.

He wrote only three German operas: *Die Entführung aus dem Serail*, *Der Schauspieldirektor*, and *Die Zauberflöte*, composed in 1791.

He left seventeen symphonies and instrumental works of all kinds.

As a performer, Mozart was one of the foremost pianists in Europe. He played very rapidly, and the speed of his left hand was particularly admirable.

Haydn himself was deeply impressed by Mozart, and made the following declaration to Leopold on one of his travels to Vienna: 'Before God and as an honest man, I tell you that your son is the greatest composer known to me either in person or by name.'

This was Mozart the *musician*, but those who understand the complexities of human nature will not be surprised to learn that this man admired by everyone for his great gifts, was not as great in other spheres. Mozart was not handsome of face, nor was his body particularly well proportioned, although curiously enough his parents were renowned for their physical beauty.

Cabanis tells us: 'It appears that the sensibilities react somewhat like a fluid, the total amount of which is fixed, and which, each time it flows in great abundance into a specific channel, diminishes proportionately in other channels.'

Mozart did not become robust as he grew up: his health was frail all his life; he was thin and pale; and although the shape of his face was out of the ordinary, his features were remarkable only in their extreme mobility. His face changed expression constantly, but indicated only the pleasure or pain he was experiencing at that precise instant. He had a habit which is often associated with simplemindedness: his body was in perpetual and restless movement and either his hands were in constant motion or his feet were tapping the floor. There was nothing extraordinary in his pastimes except for his passion for billiards. He had a billiard table at home, and would almost daily play by himself if there was no partner at hand. He was so gifted for the keyboard that his hands were clumsy in almost every other pursuit. He did not cut his food at table or, if he did so, he had much difficulty. Usually, he would ask his wife to perform this task for him.

This man who, as an artist, had reached the pinnacle of perfection at a very precocious age, was the same being who remained a child in all other aspects of life. He never learned how to govern his daily existence. He never managed to put order into his domestic affairs, money matters, or his personal pleasures. Gratification of the moment was the supreme law. His mind was constantly absorbed by a torrent of ideas that made him incapable of concentrating on what are referred to as 'serious things', with the result that Mozart needed someone all his life to take charge of his everyday affairs. His father was well aware of this weakness, and it explains why he sent his wife along with his son to Paris in 1777, as he could not obtain paid leave of absence at that time from his post in Salzburg.

But the same man, always disorganized, always playful and fun-loving, seemed to become another person from another and elevated sphere when he sat down in front of a piano. His soul was uplifted, and his whole attention was focused on the one thing for which he had been born: the *harmony of sounds*. He could pick out the slightest false note during a performance of the largest orchestra imaginable, and could point out with total accuracy the instrument that had played the false note and what sound it should have made.

When Mozart left for his trip to Berlin, he arrived very late in the evening. He had barely got out of the carriage before asking the stable boy if there was an opera being performed. 'Yes, there is: *The Abduction from the Seraglio.*'

'Charming!' answered Mozart and off he went to see the show. He placed himself in as inconspicuous a spot as possible so that no one would recognize him. But soon he was caught up in the music and the performance, at times pleased with the playing and, at others, displeased with the tempo of certain passages, or the embroidering of the actors; finally, he found himself beside the orchestra pit and when he heard a passage the conductor had decided to change, he was beside himself and, very loudly, began to inform the orchestra how the passage should be played. When the audience looked around to find out who was making all the noise, they saw a man in traveller's clothes; someone recognized Mozart and in no time the actors and musicians learned he was in the hall. Some of the artists, among them a very good soprano, were so startled by his presence that they refused to go on stage. The conductor informed Mozart of the crisis and in an instant he was backstage, praising the actors for their performance and persuading them the show must go on.

Music was his life's occupation and his favourite pastime, too. It was never a chore for him to sit down at the piano, even when he was a very young child. On the contrary, it was necessary to watch over him to make sure he did not overdo it and harm his health. Even very young, he had a marked preference for playing music at night. When he sat down at the harpsichord at nine in the evening, he would continue playing until midnight; and even then he had to be dragged away from his music, or he would go on playing preludes and variations all night long. In daily life, he was the gentlest of men; the slightest noise, however, that was made while music was playing made him extremely annoyed. He was far beyond that false (or misplaced) reticence that some artists display when begged to play. The great noblemen of Vienna often reproached Mozart for playing with the same enthusiasm for anyone who enjoyed listening to his genius.

Chapter IV

A music lover, in a city that Mozart was to visit on one of his travels, had gathered together a large group of his friends so they could enjoy hearing the famous musician. Mozart arrived, was not very talkative, and sat down at the piano. He thought he was in the company of connoisseurs, and started to play a very slow movement. The music flowed smoothly but was extremely simple, for it was his intention to edge his audience slowly into the emotions he planned to express. The assembly found it quite banal. Soon his playing became more lively and everyone found it rather pleasant. But when he switched to a severe, solemn mode that was percussive and more difficult, some of the ladies started to fidget and began exchanging critical asides; soon half the assembly was chatting loudly. The master of the house was on tenterhooks, and at last Mozart realised the effect his playing was having on the audience. He did not drop the main idea he had started to express at the outset, but now he developed it as impetuously as he could. Once again, the audience ignored him. He started to berate the assembly quite rudely but did not stop playing and, since he was speaking in Italian, no one understood what he was talking about. The audience gradually started to calm down and, when Mozart's anger had subsided, he had to laugh at his own impetuosity. He gave a more popular turn to his ideas, and ended with ten or twelve charming variations on a well-known tune. Everyone was delighted, and very few of them were aware of the little drama that had just taken place. Mozart left shortly afterwards, but invited the master of the house and a few connoisseurs to meet him that evening at his lodgings and to stay for supper. They did so and, at the first sign of a desire on their part to hear him play, he began a series of fantasies on the harpsichord. To their pleased astonishment, Mozart went on playing without pause until after midnight.

Once, an old harpsichord tuner came to replace a few strings on Mozart's travelling pianoforte. 'My good man,' said Mozart, 'tell me how much I owe you; I'm leaving tomorrow.'

The poor old man, who considered Mozart to be some sort of god, was so disconcerted that he could only manage to stammer out a few words: 'Your imperial majesty! Kappelmeister to his imperial majesty! I can't.... It's true I have come a few times to work for you.... You can pay me a few pennies.'

'A few pennies!' Mozart answered. 'Come now! A good person like yourself shouldn't get just a few pennies for his work.' And he gave the old man a few ducats.

As the man left, he was still babbling and bowing and repeating over and over: 'Ah, your imperial majesty... your imperial majesty....'

Of all his operas, Mozart liked *Idomeneo* and *Don Giovanni* best. He disliked discussing his works, or if he did speak of them, he never said very much. He said one day about *Don Giovanni*: 'This opera was not composed for the public of Vienna; it is better suited to the public of Prague, although actually I wrote it for myself and my friends.'

He worked best in the morning, usually from six or seven o'clock to ten. Then he would get out of bed. He did not compose for the rest of the day, unless he had to finish a rush job. He was always irregular in his work habits. Once he got an idea, there was no tearing him away from his work. If he was removed from the piano, he would continue composing in his friends' very midst, and would spend entire nights writing music. At other times, his spirit was so recalcitrant that he was unable to finish a score until the very instant it was supposed to be played. Once, he put off to the last moment a piece that he had been commissioned to write for a concert at the court and did not find time to write down the part he was to play. The Emperor Joseph, as he was poking through the scores of the musicians, happened to glance at the page Mozart seemed to be following and was surprised to see nothing but blank lines. He turned to Mozart and asked, 'Where is your score?' And Mozart, tapping his finger against his head, answered: 'In here.'

Another close call happened to him with the overture to *Don Giovanni*. It is generally agreed that this overture is one of Mozart's finest, yet he started working on it the night before the premier and after the final rehearsal had taken place. That evening around eleven o'clock, Mozart asked his wife to prepare a glass of punch for him and to keep him company so he would not fall asleep. She agreed to do so, and proceeded to tell him fairy tales, and strange tales of adventure that made him laugh to the verge of tears. The punch, however, was making him sleepy, so that the only time he could get any work done was while his wife was talking, and as soon as she stopped he would fall asleep. His efforts to stay awake, the switching back and forth between the waking and sleeping state, tired him to such an extent that his wife begged him to take a nap, assuring him that she would waken him in an hour's time. He slept so soundly that she let him be for two hours. Mozart had set up an appointment with the scribes for seven o'clock, and when they arrived the overture was ready. They barely had enough time to make copies for the orchestra, and the musicians were obliged to play the piece without rehearsing it. Some people claim they can hear in this music the passages where Mozart was suddenly overcome by sleep, and other passages where he wakes up with a start.

Don Giovanni was not well received when it premiered in Vienna. Shortly after the first performance, a large assembly of music lovers including Haydn were discussing the opera. Mozart did not take part. Everyone agreed that the work was admirable, rich in imagination and genius; but everyone also had criticisms to offer. All had spoken their minds except the modest Haydn. He was asked to give his opinion. 'I am not in a position to judge,' he said in his usual reticent fashion, 'but all I can say is that Mozart is the greatest composer alive today.' The subject was dropped at once.

Mozart, for his part, had much esteem for Haydn. He dedicated a series of quartets to him that are among the finest string quartets ever written. A Viennese composer, who was not without some merit, but who was nowhere near the greatness of Haydn, took malicious delight in poking through Haydn's scores in search of the tiniest error, no matter how insignificant. He would often come to see Mozart in great glee to show him the scores of symphonies or quartets he had copied and where he had detected certain errors in style. Mozart would always try to change the subject, but finally he was exasperated and said in a somewhat rude tone of voice: 'If the two of us were suddenly joined into one man, there still wouldn't be enough to make another Haydn.'

A painter, who was trying to flatter Cimarosa, told him one day that he thought he was a better musician than Mozart. Cimarosa replied curtly: 'Me better than Mozart? What would you say, sir, to a man who came up to you and told you that you were better than Raphaël?'

Chapter V

Mozart judged his own works impartially and often with a severity he would not have readily borne in others. The Emperor Joseph II was fond of Mozart, and had made him his kappelmeister, but this prince claimed he was a *dilettante*. His stay in Italy had instilled in him a liking for Italian music, and the Italians at his court lost no opportunity to fan the flames of his interest which, I believe, was quite genuine.

There was more envy than justice in their words when discussing Mozart's first attempts at the court of the emperor, and the latter, allowing others to judge for him, was easily influenced by their decisions. One day when he had just attended the rehearsal of *Seraglio*, which he himself had commissioned from Mozart, he said to him: 'My dear Mozart, all of that is too lovely for our ears; there are too many notes in it.'

Mozart answered quite curtly, 'I beg your Highness's pardon, but there are exactly the right number of notes.'

Joseph did not respond, and appeared embarrassed, but when the opera was performed, his praises were boundless. Some time later, Mozart himself was somewhat displeased with this opera; he made many corrections and rearrangements. On one occasion, while playing on the piano one of the most acclaimed airs in the opera, he said: 'This is fine in a room, but there is too much verbiage for the stage. When I composed this opera, everything seemed appropriate to me and nothing seemed too long.'

Mozart was not a person with ulterior motives; on the contrary, kindness was the mainspring of his character; he often gave without being selective and spent money freely and not always wisely.

On a trip to Berlin, King Frederick William II offered Mozart a considerable sum if he would remain at his court and take charge of the orchestra. Mozart's only answer was 'Will I have to leave my good emperor?' And yet, at that time, Mozart did not have any fixed post in Vienna. Later, one of his friends found fault with him for not accepting the king of Prussia's proposal. 'I like living in Vienna,' Mozart answered, 'and the emperor is fond of me and money doesn't interest me that much.'

And yet, as a result of strife stirred up by certain persons at court, Mozart was prompted to tender his resignation to Joseph. One word, however, from this prince who liked Mozart and his music was enough to make him change his mind. He was not worldly enough to take advantage of this favourable opportunity to ask for a fixed income. The emperor, however, soon had the idea himself to see to Mozart's financial security but unfortunately he asked a person, who disliked Mozart, what remuneration would be appropriate. The sum proposed, eight hundred florins, was more money than Mozart had ever earned. It was his salary as 'Composer of the Chamber', but he never worked in that capacity. He was once asked, in compliance with a state decree frequent in Vienna, to disclose the amount of income he received from the court. He sent the following answer by sealed letter: 'Too much for what I do, too little for what I could do.'

The music merchants, theatre managers and other business men took daily advantage of Mozart's well-known disinterest in money matters. It is for this reason that most of his compositions for piano earned him so little. He composed them to please people in his circle, those who expressed a wish to own something of his creation for their personal use. On these occasions he was obliged to take into consideration the degree of worldly power to which these persons had attained; and this explains why so many of his compositions for the harpsichord seem unworthy of him. Artaria, a

Viennese music merchant, and several of his colleagues, knew how to procure copies of these compositions, and they published them without the author's permission and without paying him any royalties into the bargain.

Chapter VI

One day, an impresario in dire straits came to see Mozart. He informed him of his sorry situation and added, 'You are the only person in the world who can save me!'

'What do you mean?' asked Mozart. 'How can I save you?'

'By writing an opera that will please the patrons of my theatre; an opera that in some respects will appeal to connoisseurs and add to your reputation; but the opera will have to be aimed mainly at the general public who does not know good music. I could get the libretto to you shortly, and the décor would be attractive; in a word, I could prepare everything as it should be if you accept my offer.'

Mozart was touched by the poor devil's request, and agreed to come to his assistance.

'What is your fee?' asked the impresario.

'You have no money,' answered Mozart, 'but listen to what I have to say: here is what we'll do to solve your problems and to make sure I can reap some benefit from my labour: I'll give the score to you only, and you will pay me what you can on the express condition that you will allow no copies to be made. If the opera is a success, I'll sell it to other theatres.'

The impresario was overwhelmed by Mozart's generosity and showered him with promises. Mozart composed the opera in record time, and in keeping with the kind of music the impresario had wished. The opera was performed; the theatre was filled to capacity every night; its success spread throughout all Germany. A few weeks later, the opera was being played at five or six different theatres and not one of them had received a copy from the indigent impresario.

On other occasions, Mozart would receive nothing but ingratitude from those he tried to help; yet, nothing could cure him of his innate kindness to persons in distress. Every time artists who had fallen on lean days came through Vienna and, not knowing anyone else, turned to him for help, he would offer them bed and board, introduce them to people who might be of assistance, and seldom allowed them to leave without first composing a concerto for their personal use. He would not even keep a copy of the music so they could be the only ones to play the concerto and thus add to their personal fame and glory.

Mozart often gave concerts at his home on Sundays. A Polish count, who came by on one such occasion, was enchanted, like the other guests, by a piece of music for five instruments that was being performed for the first time. He begged Mozart to compose a trio for flute for him when he found the time. Mozart promised to do so, on the condition the count not be in too great a hurry. Once back home, the count sent a generous sum of money to Mozart along with a very courteous letter thanking him for the pleasant time spent in his company. Mozart sent off the original score of the music for five instruments which had seemed to please the count so much. A year later he came to see Mozart, and asked about his trio.

'Sir,' said Mozart, 'I have not yet felt ready to compose something that would be worthy of you.'

'Well then,' replied the count, 'you probably do not feel ready to reimburse the money I sent you in advance for the trio.' Mozart was insulted and returned the count's money on the spot, but the count made no mention of the original score for five instruments he had received, and shortly thereafter it was published by Artaria as a quartet for harpsichord, with violin, viola, and cello accompaniment.

Mozart was quick to pick up new habits and keep them. He was very attached to his wife but her health was frail. During a long illness she suffered, Mozart would run to meet anyone who came to see her, and putting his finger before his mouth, he would make sure no one made any noise. His wife recovered, but for a long time afterwards he would approach people entering his house with his finger to his mouth, and speak to them in whispers. During his wife's illness, Mozart would sometimes go riding early in the morning, but not before leaving a note for her beside her bed and which was written up like a doctor's prescription. Here is one of them:

Good morning, my sweet friend. I hope you slept well and that nothing disturbed you. Take care not to catch cold, or hurt yourself, if you bend over. Don't be angry with the servants. Don't let anything upset you until I get back. Take good care of yourself. I'll be back at nine o'clock.

Constanza Weber was an excellent companion for Mozart, and a constant source of encouragement and advice. They had two children whom Mozart loved dearly. He had a considerable income, but his excessive spending on amusements and the disorder in his personal affairs resulted in his leaving little to his family except the glory of his name and the acclaim of the Viennese public. After his death, the Viennese sought to show their gratitude to his children for the years of enjoyment he had given them.

In the last years of Mozart's life, his health, which had always been delicate, began to decline rapidly. Like all persons of imagination, he worried about possible future misfortunes. The notion that he did not have long to live tormented him often, and his usual reaction was to work very hard and with great concentration, to the point that he sometimes forgot about everything else except his art. It often happened that, in the midst of his enthusiasm, his strength left him, and he would collapse from fatigue and have to be carried to bed. Everyone was aware that his habit of working at fever-pitch would ruin his health. His wife and friends did what they could to distract him: out of deference to them, he would accompany them on walks and visits, but his mind was elsewhere. The only thing that roused him occasionally from his moodiness was the premonition of his immanent death, a notion that always caused renewed anguish in his soul. One can see in this the same kind of derangement that Tasso experienced, the same that made Rousseau so happy in the valley of the Charmettes when the fear of his impending death drove him to embrace the only true philosophy: *carpe diem* and forget all worries. Were it not for this state of exalted sensibilities that we call genius, and which can edge into madness, perhaps there would be no art since art depends on sensitivity for its existence.

Mozart's wife, worried about the way her husband was different from other men, was determined to have people around him whom he liked and who would try to distract him when he was working too hard. Their visits pleased him but he would not stop working on his music. His friends chatted and laughed, trying to draw him into the conversation, but to no avail. When they asked him something, he would answer in a few disjointed phrases without looking up from his work.

Extreme concentration of this kind is often associated with genius, but it is by no means an infallible sign. Antoine Thomas is a case in point: is there anyone who reads his tedious collection of superlatives? And yet he was so absorbed in his meditations on the means to attain eloquence, that on one occasion at Montmorency when his groom presented him with the horse he usually rode, he offered the horse a snort of snuff. Anton Raphael Mengs was, in his time, another model of concentration, and yet he was a painter of mediocre talent, whereas Guido Reni, a great gambler, and who, towards the end of his life, would paint as many as three canvases to pay off his debts of the night before, has left works that, even when less than his best, give more enjoyment than the very best by Mengs or Carlo Maratti, both of whom were men noted for their assiduity. A woman told me once: 'Someone swore to me that I would reign forever over his soul and that I would always be the one and only mistress of his soul. And so God help me, I believe him! But what is the point since I don't like his soul?' What is the point of a man with no genius applying himself? Mozart was perhaps the most striking example in the eighteenth century of both application and genius. Georg Franz Benda, the author of *Ariadne in Naxos*, was also known for his spells of concentration.

Chapter VII

It was in a concentrated state of mind that Mozart composed *The Magic Flute*[2], *La Clemenza di Tito*, his *Requiem*, and other compositions less well known. It was while he was working on the music for *The Magic Flute* that he began to have the fainting spells we have mentioned. He was very fond of this opera, although he was not pleased by the public's infatuation with some of its music and which they insisted on hearing over and over again. The opera was performed many times, but Mozart's state of health was so poor that he could not direct the orchestra beyond the first nine or ten performances. When he was too weak to go to the theatre, he would hold his watch in his hand and imagine how events were unfolding: 'The first act is over by now,' he would point out to his friends, 'and now they're singing such and such an aria.' And then he would be overcome by the thought that he would soon have to leave all that.

A curious incident occurred which reinforced the gloomy effect of his premonitions. I would like to talk about it in some detail since we owe the famous *Requiem* to it, which is rightly looked upon as one of

Mozart's masterpieces. One day, as Mozart was plunged in deepest thought, he heard a coach pull up at his door. A stranger who had come to see him was announced. The stranger was ushered in; Mozart saw a man of mature age, very well dressed, with gracious manners and an imposing air.

'Sir,' the stranger said, 'at the request of a very important person, I have been sent to see you— '

'Who is this person?' Mozart interrupted.

'He wishes to remain anonymous,' replied the stranger.

'Well and good,' said Mozart, 'and what does he want?'

'He has just lost a loved one who will remain eternally dear to him,' the stranger answered, 'and his wish is to remember his beloved's death each year with a memorial service and he would like you to write a requiem for the occasion.'

Mozart was deeply affected by these words, the solemn tone of the stranger, and the mysterious aura that seemed to hover over the whole incident. He promised to write a requiem.

The stranger continued, 'Apply all your talent to the work as you will be composing for a connoisseur of music.'

'All the better,' said Mozart.

'How much time will you need?' asked the stranger.

Mozart replied: 'Four weeks.'

'Good. I shall return in four weeks' time. What is your fee?'

'One hundred ducats,' said Mozart, and the stranger counted out the sum on the table and left.

Mozart remained deep in thought for some time. Suddenly, he asked for pen, paper and ink, and, despite his wife's pleadings, he set to work. He continued writing feverishly for several days; he worked night and day and with a passion that increased as the days passed. His body, however, was too weak to support his efforts and one morning he lost consciousness, forcing him to suspend work for a time. Two or three days later, as his wife was attempting to take his mind off the dark thoughts depressing him, he told her quite bluntly: 'One thing is certain, the requiem I'm writing is for me. It will be sung at my own funeral service.' And nothing could rid him of this thought.

As Mozart worked on the requiem, he felt his strength ebbing daily, and the music was slower and slower in coming. The four weeks he had requested were over, and one day the same stranger appeared at his door.

'I was not able to keep my word,' said Mozart.

'Don't worry about it,' said the stranger. 'How much more time do you need?'

'Four more weeks,' Mozart answered. 'The work has aroused my interest more than I expected it would, and its design is more elaborate than I had originally planned.'

'In that case,' said the stranger, 'it is only fair to increase your fee; here are fifty ducats more.'

Mozart's astonishment increased and he said, 'Tell me who you are.'

'Who I am is of no consequence. I shall return in four weeks.'

Once the stranger had left, Mozart immediately called one of his servants and told him to follow the stranger and find out who he was. But the servant was not clever enough to pick up the trail, and the stranger vanished without a trace. Mozart became obsessed with the idea that the stranger was not human but was a being sent from the other world to warn him of his impending doom. He set to work on the requiem with even more intensity, now convinced the work was the most durable monument to his genius. Several times he again lost consciousness and his health deteriorated alarmingly. Finally the *Requiem* was completed before the four-week deadline. The stranger returned when he said he would, but by then Mozart was dead.

His life was as short as it was brilliant. He was barely thirty-six years old when he died, but in those few years he forged a name for himself that will not perish as long as sensitive souls live on earth.

A Letter Concerning Mozart

Monticello, August 29, 1814.

It follows from what has just been said, my good friend, and it seems to me to be an accurate account, that only *Figaro*, *Don Giovanni*, and *Così fan tutte* – all of which were performed at the Odéon – are the only operas by Mozart that are known in Paris.

The first observation that comes to mind about *Figaro* is that Mozart's great sensitivity has altered the fairly lukewarm sentiments that Beaumarchais ascribes to the likeable characters in the Château d'Aguas-Frescas. Count Almaviva wants, very simply, to have Suzanne, which is quite a far cry from the emotions portrayed in the aria:

> *Vedro mentr'io sispiro*
> *Felice un servo mio!*

And in the duo:

> *Crudel! perchè finora?*

This cannot be the same man in act III, scene IV of the French play who says: 'Who has chained me to this fantasy? I have tried a dozen times to free myself. Indecision plays strange tricks! If I wanted her without a struggle, my passion would strangled be.'

From this, how did Mozart arrive at his conception of the character in the opera and which nevertheless seems just right? How does one depict a contradiction in music?

In the play, one guesses that Rosine's fondness for the little page could take a more serious turn: the sweet melancholy of her soul, her reflections on the share of happiness that fate allots us, the contradictory feelings that are the harbingers of some consuming passion – all this is infinitely more developed in Mozart than in the French play. The state of soul just described has almost no words to express it fully, and perhaps this is where music has the power to depict feelings that words cannot. The arias sung by the countess are thus part of a whole new palette of colours. And the same is true for the character of Bartholo, so well delineated in the great aria:

La vendetta! la vendetta!

And Figaro's jealousy in the aria

Se vuol ballar signor Contino

is far removed from the lightness of the French Figaro. Seen from this angle, Mozart has altered the play as much as it is possible to do. I have my doubts as to whether music can truly express French *galanterie* and lightness in all the characters and during four acts; I think it would be very difficult, indeed.

Opera needs clear-cut emotions, bliss or despair. Subtle exchanges have little effect on the sensibilities, and are not conducive to meditation.

Figaro, when he describes the leap out of the window, says: 'The mad desire to jump can come over anybody at any time. Just think of how sheep like to jump over fences.' This is delightful, but only for about two or three seconds; if one repeats it to oneself once too often or scrutinizes it too closely, the charm vanishes.

I would like to see the good Fioravanti write the music for *Figaro*. In Mozart's opera, the only place where I hear a true echo of the French play is in the duo

Se a caso madama

between Susanna and Figaro. And even here, Figaro is too jealous when he says:

Udir brama il resto.

Lastly, to complete the masquerade, Mozart rounds off the ebullient events of the day with the finest church music one could possibly expect! It comes just after the word *perdono* in the last finale.

Mozart has completely altered the world created by Beaumarchais. The spirit of the play is present only in the situations; the characters are painted in romantic and emotional colours. Cherubino's character is merely sketched in the French play, but in the opera his entire soul is portrayed in the two arias

Non so più cosa son

and

Voi che sapete
Che cosa è amor

and in the duo at the end when he and the countess meet on the dark pathways of the garden, near a stand of great chestnut trees.

Mozart's opera is a sublime mixture of wit and melancholy and quite unique in its genre. Depicting tender feelings, or sad ones, can sometimes become tedious on stage but the spicy wit that is present in every situation makes this eventuality unlikely. To respect the play the way Beaumarchais wrote it, the music would have to be by Cimarosa and by Paisiello in equal doses. Only Cimarosa could give Figaro the sparkle and cockiness we find in the play. The aria that suggests this side of Figaro the best is

Mentr'io era un fraschetone
Sono stato il più felice

but it must be acknowledged that the Figaro here is a pale shadow of his French counterpart:

Non più andrai farfallone.

Even the melody of the aria is rather ordinary; its charm lies in the gradual way it unfolds.

To return to Paisiello: it suffices to recall the quintette in his *Barbiere di Siviglia*, where Bazile is told to go to bed to realize how perfectly he can portray purely comic situations without so much as a hint of warmth or emotion.

As a masterpiece of pure and tender melancholy, quite devoid of any tragic or solemn interferences, there is no equal to *Le Nozze di Figaro*.

I take much delight in imagining different artists performing in this opera: one of the Monbellis singing the role of the countess; Bassi in the role of Figaro, Davide or Nozzari playing the count; Madame Gaforinias Susanna; and another of the Monbellis in the role of Cherubino, with Pellegrini playing Doctor Bartholo.

If you have ever heard these lovely voices, you will share my pleasure in my imaginary cast; but as you know, in the realm of music, one can only speak knowingly of what is past. By dint of effort and detail I could give you an idea of Guido's *Aurore* in its performance at the Rospigliosi Palace even though you have never seen it; it would be very tedious of me, however, if I used my poetic prose in an attempt to describe, and with as many details as I have just given for *Figaro*, other operas by him like *Idomeneo* or *La Clemenza di Tito*.

One can honestly say, and without getting into extravagant exaggerations as one is constantly tempted to do when discussing Mozart, that his opera *Idomeneo* is incomparable and, contrary to what the Italians believe, I maintain it is the first opera seria, along with *La Clemenza di Tito*, to be worthy of the name.

Solemn majesty or exalted patriotism soon become tedious on the operatic stage, whereas tender emotions alone animate the characters in *La Clemenza*. What could be more sensitive than the passage where Titus asks his friend to confess his misdeed to him and tells him the emperor will learn nothing of it from the lips of the friend who is close at his side. The scene of the pardon at the end of the opera can move a confirmed cynic to tears. I saw this at Koenigsberg, after the horrible retreat from Moscow. It was in this city, after our return to the civilized world, that we attended a very good performance of *La Clemenza* and where the Russians politely allowed us to take a twenty-day rest which, I must confess, we direly needed.

One absolutely has to see *The Magic Flute* to appreciate it. The libretto, written with flights of tender fancy and unbridled imagination, is divinely attuned to Mozart's genius. I feel quite certain that if Mozart had been a writer, he would have described in detail the story of the negro, Monostatos, who comes in the silence of the moonlit night to steal a kiss from the sleeping princess. Chance has contrived something here that music lovers have seen only once before, in Rousseau's *Devin du village*. There, as in *The Magic Flute*, it can be said that the music and the words were both created by the same man.

Don Juan by Molière is imbued with romantic imagination; so many scenes are painted in true colours, from the murder of Donna Anna's father to the invitation made to the statue and its terrible words of acceptance: all of that is beautifully suited to Mozart's genius.

The musical accompaniment he gives to the statue's terrible response is a triumph in its lack of any false grandeur or any bombast. It is terror for the ear in the way Shakespeare can be terrible. Leporello's terror when he refuses to speak to the commanditore is depicted in comic fashion, which is rare for Mozart. Sensitive souls, though, will have noticed many passages full of pathos. Even the Parisians could not fail to be moved at

Ah! rimembranza amara!
Il padre mio dov'è?

Don Giovanni was not a success in Rome. Was it because the orchestra found the music difficult to play? In any case, I feel certain that one day the Romans will enjoy the opera. The story of *Così fan tutte* was made to measure for Cimarosa, but is quite against the grain of Mozart's talent.

Mozart was not one who could be playful where love was concerned. Love, for Mozart, was either bliss or despair. He has portrayed only the sentimental side of his characters and played down the role of the old sea captain and his caustic wit. When he does manage to do justice to the theme it is thanks to his superb knowledge of harmony as in the trio at the end:

Tutte fan così.

Seen from a philosophical point of view, Mozart as a person is even more amazing than as the author of sublime masterpieces. Chance has never before shown the soul of a genius so bare.

The body was of lesser importance in the remarkable blend of body and soul we know as Mozart, and whom the Italians refer to as *quel mostro d'ingegno*.

Notes

1. Mozart composed *Idomeneo* under very favourable circumstances. The Elector of Bavaria, who had always showered Mozart with favours and praise, had commissioned him to write this opera for his theatre in Munich which possessed one of the best orchestras in Germany. Mozart was at the peak of his genius: he was twenty-five years old, had fallen madly in love with Constanza Weber, a famous virtuoso, whom he eventually married. Her family was against the match, and even though Mozart's morals were above reproach, the Webers did not approve of his travels and his lack of steady employment. Mozart assiduously set out to show the Webers that even though he had no fixed position in society, he had gifts of considerable importance, and that the feelings he had for Constanza were the inspiration he needed for the moving arias he used in his operas. The deep love he felt for Constanza and the pride he had in his music resulted in an opera which Mozart always looked upon as his best, and which he often dipped into for ideas he would use in later compositions.

2. When the *Mystères d'Isis* was being performed at the Opéra de Paris, a newspaper

published a letter about it that was written by a German woman. Here is an extract:

'I went to see the *Mystères d'Isis*. The décor, the ballet sequences, the costumes, everything was lovely, but did I see Mozart's opera? Not a whit of it.

'The original version of *The Magic Flute* is what is known as a comic opera, a comedy sprinkled through with ariettas. The libretto is based on the novel by Séthos; the dialogue is alternately spoken and sung. This is the canvas upon which Mozart composed his delightful music that is so well suited to the words.

'How is it possible not to realise that by transforming this work into a grand opera, the whole thing is completely distorted? What was necessary, apparently, to render the opera worthy of your academy of music, was to introduce an extraneous recitatif all through the text; add songs and arias which, it is true, are by the same composer but do not belong in the opera nor are they in the same vein; add all kinds of other bits and pieces that eventually lead into the superb ballet sequence. The result is an ensemble that is not Mozart: the musical unity is disrupted, the overall intention is obliterated, and the spell of the opera is broken.

'Why could they not give us Mozart's music just as he wrote it? But no; the parody affects the most important musical pieces in the opera, making them lose their specific character and their original intent because rhythm, key, and significance have been altered.

'In the original German text, Papageno is a young bird catcher, cheery and naive, a bit of a bumpkin, and who is carrying, although he is ignorant of the fact, a magic flute. When he appears, he is dressed in bird feathers; he carries a cage on his back where he puts his captured birds, and a flute in his hand that he uses to lure them. A cheerful ritornelle announces his entrance, and he comes in singing:

Der Vogelfaenger bin ich, ja,
Stets lustig, heissa! hopsassa!
Ich Vogelfaenger bin bekannt
Bei alt und jung, im ganzen Land;
Weiss mit dem Locken umsugehn,
Und mich auf's Pfeifen zu verstehn.
(A gamut of flute notes.)
Drum kann ich froh und lustig Sein;
Denn alle Voegel sind ja mein.
(A gamut of flute notes.)

'This is the text Mozart received from his librettist, and which he set to music in his own inimitable fashion. Instead of the simple, cheerful words of the original, the

French librettist puts sentimental verses into the mouth of his birdcatcher. We hear of 'Mother Nature', 'Faithful Muses', and 'Cupid flying all around them'.

'All of that may be very pretty in France, but Mozart's music is not suited to it.

'To the music that Papageno sings to express his worry and doubt about finding a girl who will respond to his love, the French version sets words of philosophical musings that are far removed from the young birdcatcher's preoccupations:

Life is a journey,
Let us try to make it good, etc.

'This is not what Mozart was trying to say.

'And the same holds true for the lovely verses the birdcatcher and Princess Pamina sing together which the French version transforms into a trio:

I am going to see the lover
I adore again, etc.

'In German, this passage is a hymn to Love that is sung by two young persons, a princess and a birdcatcher, who meet each other in the middle of a wood. The passage is beautiful and touching when one thinks of the innocence, the ingenuousness and the delicate emotions of the two actors on stage.

'The same is true for the nymphs of the night who rescue the prince from a serpent that was about to attack him in his sleep. These young girls have never seen a man: their surprise, their fear are echoed in their singing.

'There is nothing like this in the trio sung by the women in the French opera.

'This is what happens over and over again: an interesting situation, full of natural and lively developments, is invariably replaced by trite and static events that seem to be the lifeblood of French opera.

'I won't mention certain arias that have been transposed, to their great disadvantage, to other keys, nor point out other changes for the worse. But I will complain about the beautiful arias and passages that have been cut out; I'm thinking in particular about a charming duo, innocently sung by two children; and another air sung by the prince and the princess after their trial by fire and water. This scene of the two lovers who both go through the perils of initiation is one of the reasons why I prefer the German text, in spite of certain baroque passages. And so we should say to the French in behalf of Mozart's honour: Your opera, the *Mystères d'Isis*, is a beautiful and noble work that is perhaps much better than our *Magic Flute*. Except that it has nothing to do with the opera by Mozart.

Wilhelmina*.'

---

* A note in the margin of the Mirbeau copy indicates that this name conceals a certain Madame Philipine de Bulow. Actually, the note was made by Winckler which means Stendhal 'borrowed' it from him.